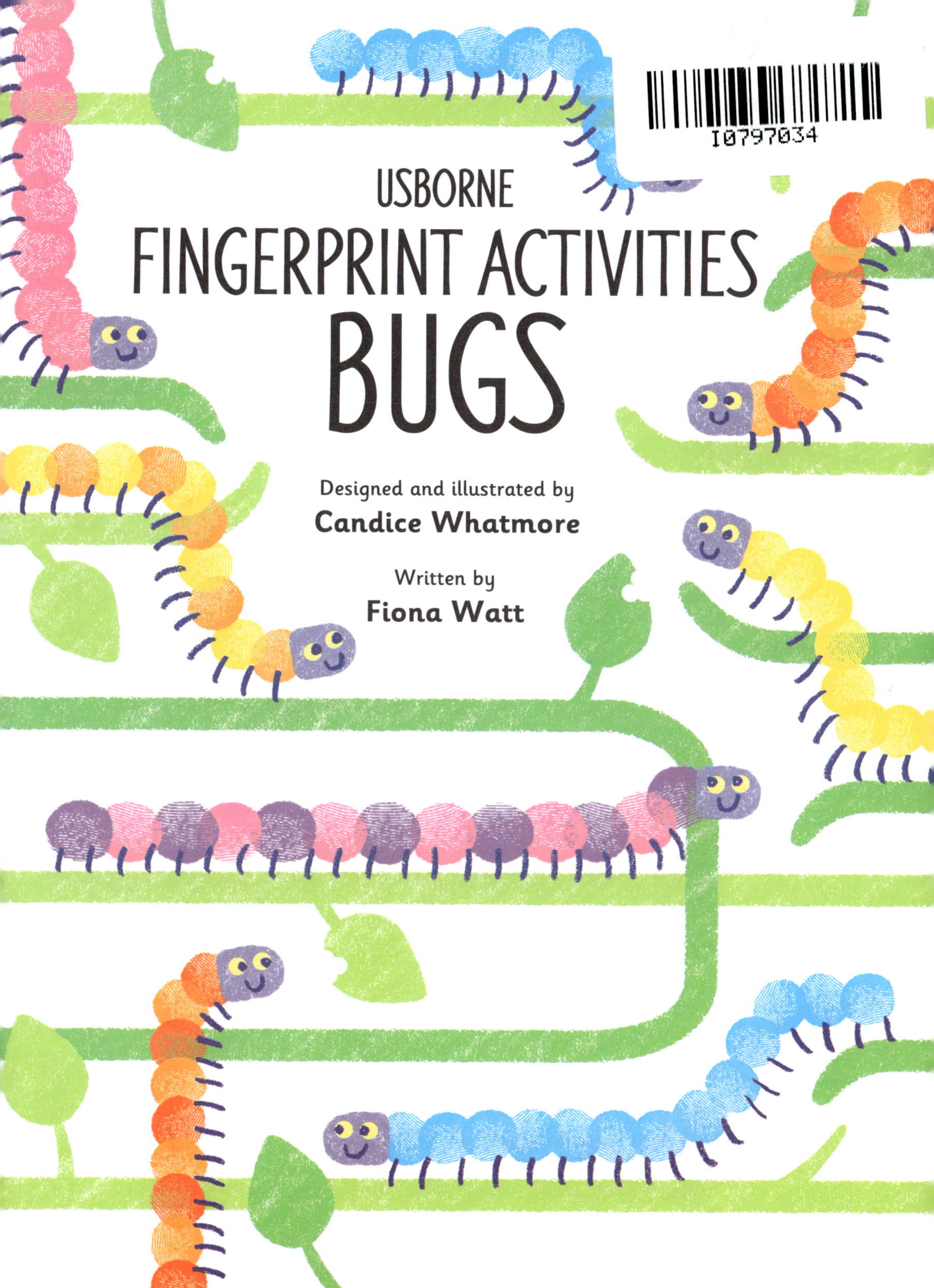

USBORNE

FINGERPRINT ACTIVITIES BUGS

Designed and illustrated by
Candice Whatmore

Written by
Fiona Watt

FINGERPRINTING TIPS

Press your finger onto one of the ink pads a few times to make sure you have a nice inky finger before printing it in the book.

Clean your inky fingers on a paper towel when you want to use a different ink. When you've finished printing, wash your hands with soap and water to get rid of any ink stains.

Try not to get the inks on your clothes or work surface as they may stain them. Don't lick your fingers - the inks won't taste very nice.

Use different fingers to make different sizes of prints. You can use the very tip of your finger to make a round print.

Finger tip

First finger

Thumb

Wait for your fingerprints to dry completely before drawing on them with felt-tip pens or crayons.

Fingerprint different sizes of spots on the bodies of these rhino beetles.

Light up the fireflies
by adding a fingerprint
to each body.

Create a swarm of grasshoppers perching on the grass.

1.

2.

3.

4.
5.

Use your middle finger and little finger to print eyes on the spider, just like those on the one below.

1.
2.
3.
Add some
flies trapped
on the web.

Fill the pages with fluttering butterflies.

Fingerprint eyes on
each praying mantis.

Add leaves to
the twigs, too.

Print lots of spots on these bugs.

Print more mosquitoes buzzing around.

1.

2.

3.

4.

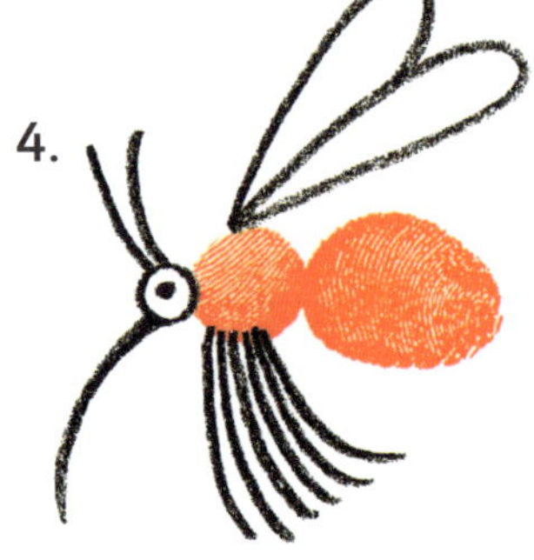

Ouch! Some of them are biting.

1. 2.

Add more bites on the skin.

Add lines of fingerprints to complete these long bugs.

Give each ant a leaf to carry back to its nest.

Add lots more bugs living on the damp forest floor.

Add bodies to the caterpillars' heads.

Fingerprint
stripes on these
strange bugs.

Cover the rosebush with tiny aphids.

1.

2.

3.

4.

Add bodies, legs and wings to all these little flies.

Use your little finger to
print raindrops in the sky...

...then add lots of wiggly worms
coming up to the surface.

The aardvark is looking for ants to eat.
Print ants scurrying around.

Add fingerprinted shells to these hungry snails.

Print lots of tiny spiders on the webs.
1.
2.
3.

Fingerprint honey bees flying around their nest.

1.

2.

3.

4.

Complete the
honeycomb
pattern on
the nest.

1.
2.
3.
4.
Fill the pages with fruit flies.

Add big eyes to these dragonflies.

Cover the bugs'
bodies with
patterns.

American
MUSTARD
mild and tasty
BEANS
n tomato sauce
SALT

1. 

2. 

3. 

4.

Oh no! Cockroaches have infested the kitchen.
Add more of them scurrying around.

Lots of moths are hovering near the lights. Add their wings.

1.

2.

3.

You could print
four wings too.

Add bodies and long legs to create pondskaters.

Buzzzz! Fill the pages with wasps.

1.

2.

3.

4.

5.

1.
2.
3.
4.
Continue filling the pages with lots and lots of little bugs.

Make millipede bodies with lines of overlapping fingerprints. Then, draw lots and lots of legs.

Decorate the
butterflies' wings.

Fill the page with lots of crazy bugs. Try to make them look as strange as you can.

Fill the centipedes' bodies with fingerprints.

Leafcutter bees cut pieces out of leaves to make their nests. Use the green ink to make holes in these leaves.

Add lots of dung beetles rolling the balls of dung.

First published in 2020 by Usborne Publishing Limited, 83-85 Saffron Hill, London EC1N 8RT, United Kingdom. usborne.com
First published in America 2020. This edition published 2025. UE.